WILDLIFE AT RISK

ENDANGERED
TIGERS

Jane Katirgis and Carl R. Green

Enslow Publishing
101 W. 23rd Street
Suite 240
New York, NY 10011
USA
enslow.com

Published in 2016 by Enslow Publishing, LLC.
101 W. 23rd Street, Suite 240, New York, NY 10011

Library of Congress Cataloging-in-Publication Data

Katirgis, Jane, author.
 Endangered tigers / Jane Katirgis and Carl R. Green.
    pages cm. — (Wildlife at risk)
 Summary: "Discusses tigers, why they are endangered, and how they are being helped"—Provided by publisher.
 Audience: Ages 11+.
 Audience: Grades 7 to 8.
 Includes bibliographical references and index.
 ISBN 978-0-7660-6906-0 (library binding)
 ISBN 978-0-7660-6904-6 (pbk.)
 ISBN 978-0-7660-6905-3 (6-pack)
 1. Tiger—Juvenile literature. 2. Endangered species—Juvenile literature. 3. Tiger—Conservation—Juvenile literature. I. Green, Carl R., author. II. Title.
 QL737.C23K394 2016
 599.75'5—dc23

                         2015010121

Printed in the United States of America

To Our Readers: We have done our best to make sure all Web site addresses in this book were active and appropriate when we went to press. However, the author and the publisher have no control over and assume no liability for the material available on those Web sites or on any Web sites they may link to. Any comments or suggestions can be sent by e-mail to customerservice@enslow.com.

Portions of this book originally appeared in the book *The Tiger*.

Photos Credits: Aditya Singh/Moment Open/Getty Images, pp.18, 31; Brian Mckay Photographyy/ Moment/Getty Images, p. 32; China Photos/Getty Images, p. 29; Creativ Studio Heinemann/Creative (RF)/Getty Images, p. 1 (borage flowers); David Soanes Photography/Moment/Getty Images, p. 1 (tiger); hudiemm/E+/Getty Images (notebook fact boxes throughout book); Hulton Archive/Hulton Royals Collection/Getty images, p. 24; Joakim Leroy/E+/Getty Images, p. 1 (palm leaf); Konrad Wothe/LOOK-foto/LOOK/Getty Images, p. 41; Lau Yan Wai/Moment/Getty Images, p. 14; Leisa Tyler/LightRocket via Getty Images, p. 35; Maria Toutoudaki/Photodisk/Getty Images (background paper texture); Photo by Steve Wilson/Moment/Getty Images, p. 38; Tim Graham/Getty Images News/ Getty Images pp. 27, 37; Tom Brakefield/Digital Vision/Getty Images, p. 7; Wolfgang Kaehler/LightRocket via Getty Images, p. 11.

Cover Credits: David Soanes Photography/Moment/Getty Images (tiger); Joakim Leroy/E+/Getty images (palm leaf); Creativ Studio Heinemann/Creative (RF)/Getty Images (borage flowers); Maria Toutoudaki/ Photodisk/Getty Images (background paper texture).

CONTENTS

Tigers at a Glance

Scientific Name

Panthera tigris. Historically, there were nine subspecies.

Endangered Subspecies (6)

Bengal (Indian), Indochinese, Siberian (Amur), Sumatran, and Malayan tigers. The South China tiger is possibly extinct in the wild because it has not been directly seen there since the 1970s.

Extinct Subspecies (3)

Caspian, Bali, and Javan tigers.

Lifespan

In the wild, 12 to 26 years; in captivity, 20 years or longer.

Adult Male:

   Length: 106–122 in (269.2–309.9 cm)

   Height: 36–44 in (91.4–111.8 cm)

   Weight: 385–570 lbs (174.6–258.6 kg)

Adult Female:

   Length: 97–105 in (246.4–266.7 cm)

   Height: 36–44 in (91.4–111.8 cm)

   Weight: 220–385 lbs (99.8–174.6 kg)

Pelage (Coat of Fur)

Orange-gold, black striped coat with white underbelly. White-and-black striped tigers are rare in the wild.

Gestation Period

93 to 111 days

Number of Young

Litters of two to seven cubs.

Diet

Hoofed mammals, such as deer and wild pigs.

Territory (Range)

Male Bengal tigers rule a territory of some 40 square miles (64.4 km^2). Females occupy smaller ranges within the male's territory.

Threats to Survival

Loss of habitat and poaching.

Current Habitat

The largest populations inhabit the forests of Southeast Asia. Smaller populations survive in the cedar forests of Northern Asia and on the island of Sumatra.

Current Population*

Today's wild tiger population is estimated at 3,200. Subspecies numbers range from 2,500 Bengal tigers to as few as 450 Siberian tigers and fewer than 400 Sumatran tigers.

Legislative Status

Most surviving tigers live in parks and reserves and are protected by endangered species laws.

*Figures represent average measurements.

chapter one

MEET *PANTHERA TIGRIS*

The scene is picturesque: a sleek and strong Bengal tiger begins to hunt as the late afternoon sun illuminates its golden coat. The tiger is king of its habitat, and it is as skilled at hunting as an Olympic gold-medalist is at attaining first place. The tiger's prowess is no match for its small weaker prey.

Noiseless on padded feet, the tiger slips closer to a group of small deer. All at once, the deer catch the tiger's scent. As they turn to run, the tiger springs into the clearing. One of the does stumbles and goes down on her knees. With two mighty bounds, the tiger is on her. Razor-sharp claws rip at the doe's flanks as powerful jaws close on her throat. Her windpipe crushed, the doe collapses and dies. The tiger quickly drags the carcass into the underbrush. Like most cats, the hunter keeps its kill to itself.

Predators

Watch a house cat as it stalks a mouse. Except for size and color, the cat could be a Bengal tiger stalking a swamp deer. This fact does not surprise scientists who study the cat family. All cats, from house pets to lions and tigers, belong to the family Felidae. House cats (*Felis catus*) and tigers (*Panthera tigris*), however, are on separate branches of the family tree.

Despite some similarities, tigers are not closely related to the long-extinct saber-toothed tiger (*Smilodon fatalis*). The tiger's closest cousins in the genus *Panthera* are lions, leopards, and jaguars. All four species can be traced to a long-ago ancestor, the

Bengal tigers, native to India, are like other subspecies of tigers in that they are keen hunters.

Proailurus lemanensis. The fossil record shows that tigers have been around for some two million years.[1]

In captivity, tigers and lions can—and do—interbreed. A female tiger that mates with a lion produces cubs called ligers. If the father is a tiger and the mother a lion, the cubs are called tigons. Like the mule, these crossbreeds cannot typically produce offspring. In California's Shambala Preserve, however, a tigon named Noelle once surprised the experts. The tigon gave birth to a cub sired by a male tiger. Actress Tippi Hedren, the preserve's founder, says that Noelle spoke both lion and tiger but spoke only tiger to her ti-tigon cub.[2]

Legends of the Tiger

Over the years, the tiger has been both admired and feared. In the 1700s, an Indian sultan's royal banner proclaimed, "The Tiger Is God."[3] Shiva, the Hindu god of salvation and destruction, is often drawn with a tiger's face. "Every creature in the jungle trembled when it sensed my approach," observed the proud tiger of R.

K. Narayan's novel, *A Tiger for Malgudi.* "Let them tremble and understand who is the master . . . of this world."[4]

Folktales, though, tend to describe the tiger in less awesome terms. One such tale, told in Thailand, explains how the tiger got its stripes. Long ago, when all tigers were a solid orange-gold color, there came a time of heavy rains. During a break in the downpour, a hungry tiger pounced on an old woodcutter.

The old man thought fast. "A great flood is coming!" he cried. "To save ourselves, we must build a bamboo raft." The slow-thinking tiger agreed, and the two went to work. When they were done, the old man pointed to the sky. "The rains are coming," he cried. "I better tie you to the raft so you can't fall off."

The tiger did as it was told. After roping the great beast to the raft, the old man fled. When at last the tiger realized that it had been tricked, it took the animal a full day to break free. As each rope broke, it left a ragged black scar on the tiger's fur. Ever since, the legend says, tigers have worn black stripes on their orange-gold coats.[5]

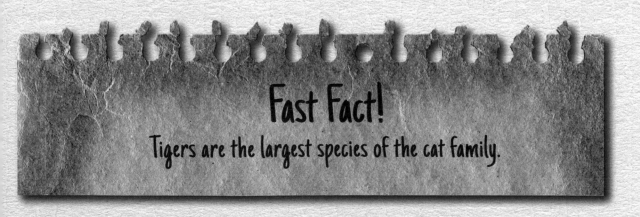

Fast Fact!
Tigers are the largest species of the cat family.

Tigers in Danger

Folktales aside, the tiger is surely not slow-witted. In real life, these powerful predators rule their wild domains, much as lions rule the African plains. A full-grown tiger can take down prey as large as water buffalo and small elephants. Only human beings, armed with axes, plows, and rifles, have been able to turn the tiger into an endangered species.

The numbers tell the story. One hundred years ago, at least 50,000 tigers lived in India. Another 50,000 roamed habitats from Siberia to Indonesia. Today the total number of wild tigers is estimated to be as few as 3,200.[6] Since the 1940s, the Bali, Caspian, and Javan subspecies have become extinct. The South China tiger, which has not been seen in the wild since the 1970s, may also be extinct in the wild.

Before the practice was banned, trophy hunters shot thousands of tigers. Today the threat of extinction comes mainly from loss of habitat, as well as the demand for tiger skins and body parts for healing remedies. From whiskers to tail, every part of the tiger is used in folk medicine throughout Asia. Until the tiger becomes worth more alive than dead, its future is in serious jeopardy. Modern medicines made from plants, rather than tiger body parts, must be promoted and made readily available. Also, the protection of natural resources needs to be encouraged and aided. Such efforts are necessary to prevent humans from further intruding on the tiger's habitat. The first step, wildlife experts insist, is to understand how the big cat lives in the wild.

A tiger hunting scene is painted on the walls at the Sisodia Palac in India.

chapter two

POWERFUL PREDATOR

"We are delighted to see a ray of hope for the tiger," proclaimed Mike Baltzer, the leader of the World Wildlife Fund's Tiger Alive Initiative. The initiative's goal is to double the wild tiger population between 2010 and 2022, the next Year of the Tiger in the Asian lunar calendar.[1] Also dubbed TX2, the goal is an ambitious one. The last count of wild tigers in 2010 estimated an all-time low for this majestic creature.

Naturalists who study the tiger share Baltzer's sense of urgency and awe. Their devoted—and often risky—work provides a detailed picture of the big cat's life cycle.

Tiger Bodies

The fossil record tells us that the tiger evolved in southern China. By modern times, tigers had spread across much of Asia. Today their habitats stretch from eastern Siberia in the north to the Caspian Sea in the west. In the south, tigers roam the forests of India and Indonesia.

In each region, the species have adapted to local conditions. Life in cold northern forests created the largest of all tigers, the Siberian. A male Siberian tiger (*P. tigris altaica*) measures some 13 feet (4 m) from its nose to the tip of its tail. Its extra thick coat helps it survive nights as cold as –49°F (–45°C). India's Bengal tiger (*P. tigris tigris*) is about two feet shorter. The Sumatran tiger (*P. tigris sumatrae*) is smaller still. Male Bengal tigers weigh about 400 pounds (181.4 kg). As in many species, the females are smaller than the males. Female Bengal tigers average 8 feet (2.4 m) in length and weigh some 300 pounds (136.1 kg). The Indochinese tiger (*P. tigris corbetti*) is smaller still. The females are usually less than 9 feet (2.7 m) long, and weigh up to 287 pounds (130.2 kg).

The tiger's body is well equipped for stalking and killing. The strong, supple muscles power the explosive charge that brings a hunt to a successful end. Long, sharp canine teeth, strong jaw muscles, and retractable claws complete the tiger's weaponry. Keen eyes and ears make up for its lack of an acute sense of smell. Like all cats, the tiger has a rough, gritty tongue. The tongue is good for grooming—and for licking the meat off bones.

The tiger's classic orange-gold and black-striped coat blends almost invisibly into dry brush. It provides good camouflage in forests and grasslands. The stripes, naturalists believe, are really stretched-out spots. White patches are found around the eyes, cheeks, legs, and on the belly. Two bright white spots behind the ears are thought to help cubs follow their mother through tall grass.[2] White Bengal tigers are often bred for zoos and circus acts, but the mutation is rare in the wild. A mutation is a genetic change in an animal's inherited traits, such as the color of its coat—for example, white instead of orange-gold. Orange-gold is the dominant, or stronger, trait, which means that it occurs more often in nature.

It is not known how often white tigers appear in the wild. In the last hundred years, only about a dozen white tigers have been seen in India. The white tiger collection in North American zoos traces its ancestry to Mohan, a single white male tiger. Mohan

Most tigers are orange-gold and black. White tigers are a result of a mutation of genes and are bred for circuses and zoos.

was captured in 1951 in central India. It did not take long for the maharajah—a king or prince of a large territory in India—who captured Mohan to figure out how to produce additional white tiger cubs. The only way was to breed Mohan with one of his own female cubs. Both the National Zoo in Washington, D.C., and the Cincinnati Zoo in Ohio can trace their white tiger line to Mohini, one of Mohan's granddaughters.[3] This process of breeding related offspring is called inbreeding, which has been known to result in birth defects.

Tiger Appetites

Meat is the mainstay of the tiger's diet—lots of meat. Tigers eat 40 to 50 hoofed mammals a year. A female Bengal tiger needs an average of 13 pounds (5.9 kg) of meat a day, which averages out to 2 to 3 percent of a tiger's body weight. If the female is raising cubs, that requirement jumps to 18 pounds (8.2 kg) a day. Over a year, that translates into 40 to 70 kills. Since most tigers succeed in bringing down their prey only one time in ten, hunting is a full-time job. In dense jungles, the ratio may fall to one kill in twenty tries. If hunting is poor, tigers fill up on edible plants, such as grass, berries, and sugar cane.[4]

Driven by their fierce appetites, tigers zero in on larger animals. One favorite is the wild ox, known as the gaur. A half-ton gaur will feed a tiger and her cubs for a week or more. Although the flesh starts to decay in a few days, tigers do not mind. They feed on a carcass until only a few scraps of bone and hide are left. If large hoofed animals are scarce, tigers hunt fish, monkeys, porcupines, peacocks, and snakes—even termites.

Each year a few tigers become man eaters. Once they lose their fear of humans, the big cats can be deadly. The champion killer was India's Champawat tigress. During a four-year killing spree from 1907 to 1911, this female tiger killed 236 people.[5] In 1937, hunter and conservationist Jim Corbett tracked down and finally killed the Champawat tigress, but not before she had killed 436 people. Today, even with far fewer tigers, the problem persists.

It is uncertain why tigers become man eaters. Some think that the tiger may have dental problems, such as broken or lost teeth, or injuries that keep them from hunting their natural prey. Humans are easier to kill than deer and other wildlife, so when a tiger is injured, it must kill what it can to survive. Wildlife experts also blame poachers for making tigers become man eaters. Poachers

Fast Fact!
A group of tigers is called an ambush or a streak.

are people who hunt tigers for their skin and body parts. The heavy poaching, some experts say, teaches tigers to view humans as enemies.

Tiger Life Cycle

Unlike the lion, the tiger is a solitary creature. A mature male Bengal tiger rules a territory as large as 40 square miles (64.4 km²). As the male patrols his range, he marks his boundaries with a spray of urine and scent. The tiger also claws deep gouges in tree trunks. As a final warning, the male lets loose a roar that can be heard 3 miles (5 kilometers) away. For mating purposes, the male allows two to seven females to occupy smaller ranges within his realm. The male largely ignores this harem, or group of females, until one of the females signals that she is ready to mate.

Scent marks and earthshaking roars bring the pair together. Courtship is a rough, noisy process. The tigers growl, circle, bite, and wrestle. At times they rear up on their hind legs and paw at each other like boxers. The pair mates many times and may take a time out to hunt together. After two or three days, each tiger goes its own way.

The tigress carries her unborn cubs for 93 to 111 days. As the time to give birth nears, the pregnant tiger beds down in a rocky crevice or under a fallen log. There the female produces a litter of two to seven 2-pound (.91 kg) cubs. In larger litters, the weaker cubs often die in the first few days. From the moment of birth, the tigress guards the blind and helpless cubs with a savage fury. At the

A mother tiger gently carries her cub by lifting it safely from behind its neck.

first sign of a threat, the new mother moves the cubs to a new den. No one is allowed close—not even the cubs' father.

For the first two months, the tigress leaves the den only to hunt. At about eight weeks of age, the cubs will start eating meat. However, they will not wean themselves from their mother until about three to six months of age. As the cubs grow larger, the female allows them to tag along on hunts. When the female makes a kill, she calls the cubs to share the bounty. Unlike a lioness, the tigress allows the cubs to eat first. By six months, the growing, playful cubs are ready to start survival lessons. The mother may begin by disabling a deer.

Then she calls the cubs to finish the kill. Six months later, the cubs graduate to stalking their own game. Unlike most cats, tigers love to swim. If a cub holds back during swimming lessons, the tigress is likely to drop it into the water.[6] Being a good swimmer can be an advantage for a tiger. Tigers are ambush hunters. Often a tiger will wait in the tall grass along a river or lake for deer and other animals to come get a drink.

Two-year-olds range farther and farther away. The tigress, in turn, is ready to mate again. After she gives birth, she chases off the grown cubs if they try to visit the new litter. Female cubs often settle near their mothers, who shift their own ranges to make room. A male cub faces a sterner test. Instinct drives him to try to take over an older male's territory. Most male cubs fail, and some die in the attempt. By the time the young male is four, he may be strong and clever enough to win this crucial battle.[7]

In a typical litter, half the cubs perish before their second birthday. Intruding older males kill some. Others drown in floods or die from injuries or disease. All too often, cubs and adults alike fall victim to the greatest threat of all—human beings.

chapter three

FIGHTING FOR SURVIVAL

Despite a 1993 ban on trading tiger parts, there is a large black market for tiger bones and skins. They are sold alongside traditional Chinese medicines in street markets. The powdered bones are sold as a treatment for typhoid fever and rheumatism. Tiger teeth are consumed for asthma, and tiger brain is said to be a cure for acne. Pelts sell for $20,000, and a tiger paw can fetch as much as $1,000.[1]

The sale of tiger parts outrages conservationists. Because tigers are protected by law, the market is mostly underground. High profits help drive the trade. A poacher can earn thousands of dollars by selling the pelt, body parts, and bones to a dealer.

The people who use tiger medications are certain they work. "We're not trying to kill tigers," says folk medicine expert David Choy. "We're trying to save human lives. The laws . . . are good for tigers but not for people."[2] Choy's claims fill animal lovers with dread—and poaching is not the only threat to tigers.

Natural Threats

For all their size and power, tigers do succumb to natural causes. Some big cats die of wounds and broken bones. They suffer the injuries in fights with rivals, falls, and while hunting. Even a minor injury can be fatal. A cub that tackles a porcupine is likely to wind up with a quill stuck in its lip. If the wound becomes infected, the cub will weaken and die. Tigers also drown in floods and perish in forest fires. Disease can play a role, as well. Canine distemper, for example, killed hundreds of Tanzania's lions in 1994. A similar outbreak could wipe out a wild tiger population.

Today's tigers also face danger from a less visible threat. Suppose that a park's population has dwindled to forty tigers. As a rule, only sixteen or so will produce cubs. Genetic diversity is lost as fathers mate with daughters and mothers mate with sons. In time, fewer cubs will be born. Those that do survive are likely to be less successful as adults because inbreeding weakens a species. Geneticist Steve O'Brien explains, "Variation is good, because . . . it provides flexibility of the species to adapt to changes."[3] Zoos that

Fast Fact!

Rare white tigers carry a gene that is only in the cells of about one in every 10,000 tigers.

breed tigers do what they can to promote genetic diversity. When choosing a mating pair, breeders try to match a female with a male from a different region.

Tiger Habitat

The human population of Asia has quadrupled during the last one hundred years.[4] Feeding and clothing all those people puts a severe strain on natural resources. Animal prey and predators vanish as villagers scour the countryside for game. Naturalist George Schaller once asked some villagers in Laos if there were Indochinese tigers nearby. He knew that the big cats were once common in the region. "Yes, one came by here a year ago," they told him.[5]

A typical battle in the war for habitat can look like this: The conflict begins with a long drought. As their fields shrivel, villagers drive their livestock into the reserve to graze. The herds soon overgraze the grasslands, leaving the park's deer, wild boar, and gazelles little to eat. Looking for prey, the local tigers turn to the villagers' cattle, water buffalo, and goats. To protect their animals, the herders strike back with guns, traps, and poison. Rather than stop the villagers, the reserve's guards step aside and allow what amounts to an organized slaughter of tigers.[6]

Since 1900, tiger habitats—and tiger populations—have been reduced by about 95 percent. All across Asia, prime forest has been turned into barren wasteland. The culprits include heavy logging, overgrazing, dam building, and erosion. Adding to the damage, cattle sometimes infect wild deer herds with viral diseases. As their prey disappears, tigers move elsewhere—or vanish.

Fast Fact!

Ninety percent of the time, a tiger hunting its prey results in failure and the prey escapes.

Man Versus Tiger

Alone and unarmed, a human is no match for a tiger. Give the human a high-powered rifle, a vial of poison, or a steel trap, and the tiger is still dangerous, but now the odds favor the human. If the human is a skilled poacher, there is a good chance the tiger will be killed. If a culture values wildlife less than the animal's value in the marketplace, the killing will go on until there are no more tigers.

The struggle between man and tiger was not always so uneven. A hundred years ago, tigers killed hundreds of people each year. To protect villagers, Indian rulers organized tiger hunting expeditions. When the British came to India, army officers took up the challenge. Mounted on elephants or perched high in the trees, they shot tigers by the thousands. During a four-year span in the 1850s, one sharpshooter killed ninety-three tigers. Only when the tiger population fell to alarmingly low numbers in the 1960s did the government ban hunting. To protect the surviving tigers, parks and reserves were set aside.[7]

The killing reached new heights in China after World War II. Communist leader Mao Tse-tung needed land for new farms, factories, and villages. To clear the way, Mao declared that tigers were an "enemy of the People." The slaughter that followed almost wiped out the Chinese tiger (*P. tigris amoyensis*) and put many tiger parts on the market. As a side effect, with tiger bone and parts plentiful, the demand for tiger medicines shot up. When the supply of Chinese tiger parts ran low, high prices inspired a surge

Since this tiger hunting party photograph was taken in India around 1923, humans have become the tigers' number one threat.

in poaching in India and Sumatra. Only in recent years have the Chinese taken steps to save their few remaining tigers.

Today illegal hunting and poaching endanger all wild tigers. Naturalists explain that for every ten tigers killed, another fifteen are likely to die. If a villager poisons a nursing mother, her young cubs are unlikely to survive. Next, poachers might kill the old male who ruled a forty-square-mile realm. His death opens the way for younger males to compete for his title. The winner will try to kill the old ruler's male cubs so he can father his own litters.

Threatened from all sides, the tiger is truly an endangered species. The one-sided battle might have been lost long ago if not for a worldwide save the tiger campaign.

chapter four
SAVING THE TIGER

The light began to dawn in the late 1960s. Unless something was done quickly, the tiger would soon be extinct. Critics, from barefoot villagers to penny-pinching government officials, said the price was too high. "Tigers eat people," they grumbled. "Who needs them?"

Operation Tiger

The news that tigers are endangered was slow in catching the world's notice. At last, in 1972 the World Wildlife Fund (WWF) launched a save the tiger campaign. Money poured in for Operation Tiger as the public awoke to the threat. Soon women who wore tiger fur coats were being booed as they walked down the street.[1] Countries large and small agreed to stop importing and exporting endangered species.

India, home of the Bengal tiger, kicked off Project Tiger in 1973. Prime Minister Indira Gandhi signed the law that set up the country's first wildlife reserve, called Bandipur National Park. Ranthambhore National Park and other reserves followed.

Tourists have the good fortune to see a female Bengal tiger up close in Ranthambhore National Park..

Next came the hard day-to-day work. Roads had to be built, and villagers had to be moved to new homes. Guards enforced new rules that outlawed hunting and logging. Fines were handed out to farmers who let their herds graze in the reserves. By 1998, India could point with pride to twenty-five parks and reserves. As other Asian countries set up their own reserves, tigers staged a modest comeback.

Laws to Protect the Tiger

The fight to save the tiger extends far beyond Asia. Many governments have been writing laws that add muscle to the enforcement movement. One major victory came in 1973. With United Nations backing, more than 120 countries signed the CITES treaty. CITES stands for the Convention on International Trade in Endangered Species of Wild Fauna and Flora. The agreement puts strict controls on the sale of endangered plants and

Customs officials in Tibet prepare to hand over confiscated wild animal skins. People can help save the tiger by reporting the sale of tiger products to the local police.

animals. Nations that violate the rules can be cut off from markets or denied loans.

Americans have played a key role in defending the tiger. Congress helped by passing the Endangered Species Act in 1967. The act provides fines of up to $25,000 and six-month jail terms for anyone who kills or sells an endangered plant or animal. In 1994, the Rhinoceros and Tiger Conservation Act made the act easier to enforce. The new law also opened the door to using tax dollars for rhino and tiger conservation. The business world joined in as Exxon Oil kicked off a fund-raising drive. (Exxon often uses an image of a tiger in their advertisements.) Caught up in the campaign to save the tigers, Americans whipped out their checkbooks. Tiger conservation groups, fueled by the influx of cash, redoubled their efforts.

Wildlife experts agree that passing laws and giving money are helpful first steps. The harder work, they say, must be done on the ground. Setting up tiger reserves is a good step, but the reserves must support a healthy prey population. Antipoaching laws are good, but only if they are enforced. Banning livestock from the forest is good, but only if villagers are given better ways to feed their herds. In short, protecting the tiger needs a balanced, long-term commitment.

A National Park Case Study

Ranthambhore National Park in north-central India is a well-known tiger reserve. The park sprawls across 150 square miles

Once tigers live in captivity, they may never be released into the wild.

(241.4 km²) of upland forests and grasslands.[2] Peacocks call from crumbling hilltop forts that once guarded a local ruler's game preserve. Spotted deer and wild boar drink at the park's three lakes. A sign at the railway station welcomes visitors to the City of Tigers.

Project Tiger reached Ranthambhore in 1973. Game warden Fateh Singh saw that only a handful of tigers still roamed the park. Strong measures were needed. Using force when persuasion failed,

Fast Fact!

A tiger has brighter eyes than any other animal in the world.

Singh moved entire villages out of the park. Next, his guards kept local herdsmen from grazing their livestock in the park. This tough approach upset the local people. Denied access to the forest, they saw an age-old way of life vanishing.

Indian conservationist Valmik Thapar saw the problem clearly. "It is no longer enough to police the tiger forests of the world," he writes. "Legislation to protect the forests has to be supported by the people who live in and around them. Only if this happens do the forest and its wildlife have a chance of surviving."[3] To enlist that support, Thapar formed the Ranthambhore Foundation. The foundation's experts introduced the villagers to new methods of conserving water and soil. They encouraged farmers to plant trees and raise new crops. Some of the crops fed village families. Other crops produced fuel for cook fires and fodder to feed domestic animals.[4]

For a time, the two-pronged approach seemed to pay off. In the mid-1980s, a report noted that as many as forty tigers were living in the park. Then nature took a hand. A seven-year drought drove herdsmen into the park in search of grass for their livestock. This time, Fateh Singh was not there to turn them back. His no-nonsense methods had cost him his job. To make matters worse, the poachers returned. By the late 1990s, the number of tigers in the park had dwindled to twelve.[5] By 2014, however, the number was back up with as many as sixty-one tigers possibly living in the park.[6]

chapter five

A Look to the Future

The countdown to extinction clock is ticking. As wildlife expert John Seidensticker puts it, "Tigers won't ultimately be safe until they're worth more alive than dead."[1] But how can conservationists make that happen when a single tiger pelt can sell for $20,000?

Tiger Populations

At first glance, the estimate that 3,200 tigers survive in the wild may sound hopeful. Several troubling facts hint at a less positive future. At least 100,000 tigers once roamed freely in Asia. In 1931, India was home to 131 million people. By 2014, the population had raced past 1.2 billion people. The rising tide of humans competes with wildlife for space, food, and fuel. Solitary free-ranging tigers are hard to count. Wildlife experts worry. They fear that park officials (whose jobs may depend on keeping tigers safe) are reporting "ghost" tigers and lying about the total number.[2] Even the widely used bottom-line figure of 3,200 wild tigers may be too high.

Elephants are used to track tigers inside Baghavahn National Park.

Captive Tigers

The big cats that are so elusive in the wild are easy to find in cages. One estimate puts the number of captive tigers at about 2,800. Caged tigers are common in zoos, safari parks, carnivals, and sanctuaries. Many sanctuaries have rescued tigers from owners who could not handle it when their cute little cubs grew up to be scary 400-pound (181.4 kg) adults.[3]

Some people look at captive cubs and say, "Raise the cubs to adulthood then return them to the wild!" If the cure were that simple, Asia's reserves would be filled with tigers. As zoologist Valmik Thapar points out, captive tigers do not learn how to hunt. Set free in the wild, they lack the skills needed to bring down wild prey. Driven by hunger, they may turn to feeding on domestic cattle—or human beings.[4]

Even in cages, captive tigers aid their own cause. A public that learns to admire the tiger's grace and beauty is more likely to pitch in to help save it. Zoos also work to safeguard genetic diversity. Mating females with males from different bloodlines produces active, healthy cubs. These cubs, in turn, will help carry on the species. One organization, The Tiger Missing Link Foundation of Tyler, Texas, is working to identify all the subspecies that are in captivity in the United States. Tigers whose parents were both of the same subspecies are purebred and vital to the success of conservation programs.

Darker chapters in the story of captive tigers exist, too. There are twenty tiger farms in China where tigers are raised in small cages and enclosures. The tiger farmers use the animals for their

People from all over the world are coming together to save the tiger. India has twenty-five parks and wildlife reserves dedicated to protecting these animals.

Fast Fact!

A tiger's roar can be heard as far as 3 miles (5 km) away.

parts. For example, one of the gift shops at the Xiongsen Tiger and Bea Mountain Village in Guilin, China, sells bone-strengthening wine made from tiger bone for $132 a bottle.[5]

Hope for the Future

In the end, the fight to save the tiger hinges on a few basic facts. There are fourteen Asian countries where tigers live in the wild. In some of these countries, it is taken for granted that the forests will always exist. As more humans are born there, villagers put greater stress on wild habitats. Saving the wild tiger, therefore, means safeguarding wildlife reserves. As zoologist Alan Rabinowitz puts it, "There can be no chipping away at the edges, no human settlements . . . no commercial exploitation." The reality, he says, is that "forest guards must be better paid . . . and better trained and better armed than the poachers. Otherwise the battle is lost from the beginning."[6]

Reforming the folk medicine market, experts say, will further cut poaching. Roots and herbs can replace the tiger parts used to treat illnesses. Insomniacs need not depend on tiger claw broth for relief. Coptis root and wild jujube seed could work just as well. Cork tree bark can replace powdered tiger bone to treat joint pain. A toothache can be relieved with ginseng instead of tiger whiskers. As more and more people switch to plant remedies, the market for tiger parts will shrink.

Fast Fact!

A hungry tiger can eat as much as 60 pounds (27 kg) in one night.

Take Action

Everyone can help the tiger fight for survival. No matter where you live, you can help save the tiger and other endangered species. Share what you have learned about tigers. Get out the word about endangered species. You can start with your family and friends. Tell them not to buy tiger products.

Alert police if you see tiger products on sale. Warn buyers and sellers alike that they are risking heavy fines or even jail. Also, support campaigns to raise money for conservation efforts, such as Project Tiger. Conservation groups raise money worldwide and work with local officials to help save endangered species. Finally, write or e-mail your elected officials. Ask them to do more to protect the tiger and other endangered species.

Zero Poaching and TX2

In February 2015, representatives from thirteen Asian countries signed on for immediate actions to stop tiger poaching. At the Zero Poaching Symposium, conservationists reinforced their goals by joining forces to put an end to the illegal action of poachers. They will improve training and support for rangers in the field, and they will work harder to collaborate in the fight against this threat to the endangered tiger.[7]

In 2016, the halfway point in the TX2 plan, there will be an interim count of the number of tigers in the wild. As Michael Baltzer said regarding the actual current count of tigers in the wild, "We don't know. The last globally acknowledged estimate is 'as few

In the past, the biggest threats to tiger cubs were injury or disease. Now it is human beings who cause the loss of the tigers' habitat and hunt the species for its different parts.

as 3,200 in 2010. . . . [and the surveys conducted in 2016, 2020, and 2022 will allow us to] know where we are on the road to 2022."[8] Baltzer and many others hard at work on the issue are hoping that the news will be good.

Will the conservation efforts pay off? The future is clouded. Humans are populating the planet at an alarming rate, and they need places to live, food to eat, and jobs to support them. Traditional customs, such as using tiger parts for medicines and tiger pelts for rugs, are difficult for people to stop doing. In the midst of the tumult, tigers require space and solitude. If humans cannot guarantee those basic needs, the wild tiger may be doomed.

Chapter Notes

Chapter 1. Meet *Panthera tigris*

1. "The Evolution of the Felids," *Forever Tigers,* n.d., <http://www.forevertigers.com/evolution.htm> (February 10, 2015).

2. Ibid.

3. Peter Matthiessen, *Tigers in the Snow* (San Diego, Calif.: Lucent Books, 1999), p. 14.

4. Quoted in Michael Nichols and Geoffrey C. Ward, *The Year of the Tiger* (Washington, D.C.: National Geographic Society, 1998), p. 2.

5. Alan Rabinowitz, *Chasing the Dragon's Tail: The Struggle to Save Thailand's Wild Cats* (New York: Anchor Books, 1991), pp. 194–195.

6. World Wildlife Fund. "Tigers," 2015, <http://www.worldwildlife.org/species/tiger > (February 10, 2015).

Chapter 2. Powerful Predator

1. World Wildlife Fund. *We Are Working to Double Wild Tigers by 2022,* "About TX2," 2015. <http://tigers.panda.org/tx2/> (February 10, 2015).

2. K. Ullas Karanth, *The Way of the Tiger: Natural History and Conservation of the Endangered Big Cat* (Stillwater, Minn.: Voyageur Press, 2001), p. 48.

3. Ronald L. Tilson, "White Tigers," *5 Tigers: The Tiger Information Center,* n.d., <http://www.5tigers.org/> (Oct. 7, 2002).

4. Michael Nichols and Geoffrey C. Ward, *The Year of the Tiger* (Washington, D.C.: National Geographic Society, 1998), p. 32.

5. World Wildlife Fund.

6. Sankhala, pp. 76–77.

7. Karanth, p. 72.

Chapter 3. Fighting for Survival

1. Andrew Jacobs, "Tiger Farms in China Feed Thirst for Parts," *New York Times,* February 12, 2010, <http://www.nytimes.com/2010/02/13/world/asia/13tiger.html?_r=0 > (February 10, 2015).

2. Cory J. Meacham, *How the Tiger Lost Its Stripes: an Exploration into the Endangerment of a Species* (New York: Harcourt Brace & Co., 1997), p. 147.

3. Ibid., p. 8.

4. World Population Statistics, *Asia Population 2013,* May 20, 2013, <http://www.worldpopulationstatistics.com/asia-population-2013/ > (February 10, 2015).

5. Michael Nichols and Geoffrey C. Ward, *The Year of the Tiger* (Washington, D.C.: National Geographic Society, 1998), p. 33.

6. Matthiessen, p. 81.

7. Kailash Sankhala, *Tiger! The Story of the Indian Tiger* (New York: Simon & Schuster, 1977), p. 90.

Chapter 4. Saving the Tiger

1. Simon Barnes, *Tiger!* (New York: St. Martin's Press, 1994), p. 128.

2 Quoted in Michael Nichols and Geoffrey C. Ward, *The Year of the Tiger* (Washington, D.C.: National Geographic Society, 1998), p. 44.

3. Valmik Thapar, *The Tiger's Destiny* (London: Kyle Cathie Ltd., Publishers, 1992), p. 168.

4. Peter Matthiessen, *Tigers in the Snow* (San Diego, Calif.: Lucent Books, 1999), pp. 80–81.

5. Stanley Breeden and Belinda Wright, Through the Tiger's Eyes: a Chronicle of India's Wildlife, (Berkeley, Calif.: Ten Speed Press, 1996), p. 153.

6. TNN, Two More Cubs Spotted in Ranthambore, *The Times of India,* May 29, 2014, <http://timesofindia.indiatimes.com/city/jaipur/Two-more-cubs-spotted-in-Ranthambore/articleshow/35694718.cms> (February 10, 2015).

Chapter 5. A Look to the Future

1. Quoted in Michael Nichols and Geoffrey C. Ward, *The Year of the Tiger* (Washington, D.C.: National Geographic Society, 1998), p. 45.

2. Simon Barnes, *Tiger!* (New York: St. Martin's Press, 1994), p. 109.

3. Ibid., pp. 84–87.

4. Cory J. Meacham, *How the Tiger Lost Its Stripes: an Exploration into the Endangerment of a Species* (New York: Harcourt Brace & Co., 1997), pp. 24–25.

5. Andrew Jacobs, "Tiger Farms in China Feed Thirst for Parts," *New York Times,* February 12, 2010, <http://www.nytimes.com/2010/02/13/world/asia/13tiger.html?_r=0 > (February 10, 2015).

6. Alan Rabinowitz, *Chasing the Dragon's Tail: the Struggle to Save Thailand's Wild Cats* (New York: Anchor Books, 1991), pp. 226–227.

7. World Wildlife Fund. "Zero Poaching Symposium: Closing Ceremony," *WWF International,* February 6, 2015, <http://tigers.panda.org/nepal/zero-poaching-symposium-closing-ceremony> (February 10, 2015).

8. World Wildlife Fund, "India Reports Nearly 30% Rise in Wild Tiger Population," January 20, 2015, <http://www.worldwildlife.org/stories/india-reports-nearly-30-rise-in-wild-tiger-population> (Feburary 10, 2015).

Glossary

black market—Buying and selling that is against government rules.

captive—Being confined or held in a safe place.

carcass—The body of a dead animal.

Chinese medicine—Traditional medical techniques based on more than 2,000 years of use. They include herbal medicine, acupuncture, and exercise.

conservation—The protection of plants, animals, and natural resources.

endangered—In danger of becoming extinct and not existing on earth anymore.

extinction—The death of an entire group, or species, of living things.

gene—A part of a cell that controls traits and characteristics, such as eye color, in a living thing.

poacher—A person who kills or steals wild animals illegally.

population—The total number of people, animals, or plants living in a specific area.

predator—An animal that hunts and eats other animals for food.

rheumatism—A disease of the joints that causes stiffness and pain.

species—A group of animals or plants that have similar features. They can produce offspring of the same kind.

threatened—A group of animals that is close to becoming endangered.

typhoid fever—A serious disease that causes high fever, headaches, and a rash.

Further Reading

Books

Baillie, Marilyn, Jonathan Baillie, and Ellen Butcher. *How to Save a Species.* Toronto: Owlkids Books, 2014.

Charman, Andy. *I Wonder Why Dinosaurs Died Out and Other Questions About Extinct and Endangered Animals.* New York, N.Y.: Kingfisher, 2013.

Claus, Matteson. *Animals and Deforestation.* New York, N.Y.: Gareth Stevens Publishing, 2014.

Kitson, Jazynka. *Mission: Tiger Rescue.* Washington, D. C.: National Geographic Children's Books, 2015.

Riddolls, Tom. *Tiger.* New York, N.Y.: Weigl Publishers, Inc., 2014.

Winter, Steve. *Tigers Forever: Saving the World's Most Endangered Big Cats.* Washington, D.C.: National Geographic Society, 2013.

Yolen, Jane. *Animal Stories: Heartwarming True Tales from the Animal Kingdom.* Washington, D.C.: National Geographic Children's Books, 2014.

Web Sites

fws.gov/international/animals/tigers.html
U.S. Fish and Wildlife Service's information about tigers.

wcs.org/saving-wildlife/big-cats/tiger.aspx
The Wildlife Conservation Society's facts about endangered tigers.

worldwildlife.org/species/tiger
Wealth of information on endangered and threatened animals.

Index